The best Spanish Dishes

offers you varied and delicious traditional Spanish recipes. For those who cannot cook and wish to become initiated in the art of cooking in a convenient, simple way. Follow the instructions and tips in this book and you will enjoy learning to prepare the best of Spain's culinary riches.

EDITORIAL EVEREST, S. A.

Madrid • León • Barcelona • Sevilla • Granada • Valencia
Zaragoza • Las Palmas de Gran Canaria • La Coruña
Palma de Mallorca • Alicante • México • Lisboa

Spain, the ancient Hispania, has always been and still is a country clearly set apart from the rest of Europe. A wall of mountains, the Pyrenees, separate it from the rest of the continent, and for this reason, although politically divided on more than one occasion, it has always enjoyed a well defined geographical unity; it would seem as if even metereological phenomena such as cyclones and anticyclones were aware of this and respected the singular nature of this land, acting as they do, almost systematically, in a different way here than in more northern latitudes.

It is a unit, that's true, but it is also a kaleidoscope, or if you prefer, a mosaic: there are mountains which are always snow-covered, with shady valleys and wooded slopes; and there are rocky mountains bereft of vegetation which seem more like the Moon; there are high tablelands with extreme temperatures, and there are also rich, fertile plains; there are large rivers which flow placidly and others in which the waters rush tumultously along narrow canyons. Some lands are cold, others are as hot as those of Africa; some are misty and damp; others arid, almost desert-like; even on the coast, the vast beaches of white, golden or grey sand alternate with the sheerest cliffs. Consequently, Spanish gastronomy - and its cuisine, which is its most genuine form of expression -, due to the fact that it is a reflexion of the climate, the geography and

Olive oil is essential to what could be called the trilogy of Mediterranean Spanish cuisine, namely its salads and sauces, its fried fish and fish stews, and the rice dishes.

the idiosyncrasy of the inhabitants of the country and moreover constitutes a kaleidoscope of races and cultures, embodies, on the one hand, the singularity of a clearly defined entity, and on the other, the variety of its natural regions and, within these, its local areas.

Spanish cuisine therefore has certain common characteristics which, with slight variations, appear in all the regional cuisines, and it also has a great many specialities, those dishes which are usually called *typical or topical* ('topical' in the sense of a cliché) of a certain area, or of just one town, and which are sometimes unknown even by the inhabitants of almost neighbouring localities. Nevertheless, the quality of many of them, and their fame,

has spread beyond their limited original geographical range, and they have been incorporated into the heritage of what could be considered genuine national cuisine. Some of them have gone even further, and it could be said, without chauvinist exaggeration, that in cases such as *paella* or potato omelette (*tortilla de patata*), they could currently be considered *world heritage*. On considering the gastronomic variety of Spain, the most ancient of the administrative or political divisions to which the country has been subjected throughout its history is the perhaps most appropriate and should be used as a reference when attempting to group its most characteristic culinary specialities. I refer, obviously, to that made by the Romans between *Hispania*

Citerior, closest to the *Mare Nostrum* and *Hispania Ulterior*, that of the rivers which flow into the Ocean or into the Bay of Biscay. In other words, Mediterranean Spain and Atlantic Spain.

Mediterranean Spain

One product characterizes its cuisine: oil. Olive oil, naturally, as no other oil can be referred to as such if it is not preceded by a name which identifies it and declares which seed it comes from. Olive oil is present in almost all its dishes; we find it even «unborn», in our hors d'oeuvres (*tapas*), in its original form of olives, black, green or purple; whole, crushed or split; in brine, with aromatic herbs, dried or in sea salt, or stuffed with anchovies or vegetables, heralds of any light meal or feast from Cádiz to Gerona.

Olive oil is essential to what could be called the trilogy of Mediterranean Spanish cuisine, namely its salads and sauces, its fried fish and fish stews, and the rice dishes.

Spain was the gateway, or rather the majestic portal, through which the vegetables from America entered Europe. They became acclimatized on the shores of the Mediterranean, so that it could be said that they are native, and moreover, they improved considerably: the peppers lost part of their fiery spirit, and the tomatoes their original acidity, and both vegetables gained in colour,

pulp, size and firmness, and became essential elements of our salads. They were joined by the aubergines brought from the east by the Arabs, and the indigenous lettuces and onions. Nowadays Spanish salads are as attractive to the palate as they are to the eye, as they are like refreshing symphonies of flavours and colours.

Abundant olive oil, vinegar in small doses and salt to taste, these are the ingredients which dress our salads. They need nothing more; butter and mustard are strangers to us, as are many of those herbs known as sauce herbs, usually found beyond the Pyrenees and absent in our fields, as they do not resist the Mediterranean sun. Neither do butter or mustard form part of the popular sauces of the Hispanic Mediterranean, as olive oil is the protagonist in all of them: *ajoaceite or allioli* (literally 'garlic and oil'); Mayonnaise or Mahonnaise (we shall not dwell upon the mystery of whether its homeland was Menorca or Bayonne); salsa *marinera*; vinaigrette; *romescu* and many more.

Probably garlic mayonnaise or *allioli* is the most characteristic of the whole coast; it does not belong to us exclusively, that's true, as this worthy sauce, with other similar designations, is enjoyed in France, Italy and Greece, but the fact that it is shared does not diminish its gastronomic glory. In its most original version, it is merely a mixture of garlic and oil,

rather too strong for the palate, therefore it is made milder by adding an egg yolk to the mixture; thus achieving a rather smooth taste which goes perfectly with all kinds of roast meats, cooked or raw vegetables and even with rice and fish dishes.

With regard to fish, the great treatises on culinary art distinguish generically several ways of preparing it; they mention boiling, frying, charcoal grilling, au gratin and others, but they seldom refer to the most popular, the most traditional form of preparation on the Spanish Mediterranean coast: the stew or casserole (*caldereta*), *suc* or *suquet*, which also receives other colloquial names.

In fact, all these culinary preparations are variations on the same theme - that of the combination of oil and fish. Any variety of the latter can be used to great success, with the necessary accompaniment of other select ingredients, such as vegetables, parsley and perhaps a spice. In all cases, it is based on the *sofrito* (lightly fried vegetable mixture), as the *sofrito* is the basic operation of the culinary technique of the whole Mediterranean area. A technique which was already familiar to sailors and fishermen in Homer's era: the oil is heated in a pan, then the crushed or chopped vegetables are added, which in ancient times were garlic and onions, the tomato not having come onto the scene until centuries later; perhaps a few pine kernels, which are a Hellenic tradition, and the *sofrito* is ready. It is not exactly frying, nor boiling, and it requires skill, as the success of the dish will depend on its quality; it also requires time, as it is necessary to achieve a perfect mixture of all the ingredients which go to make up the *sofrito*, and to this mixture the fish will be added, generally those which can be cut into slices. The contact between the fish and the oil will be brief but intimate, after which the water will be added, or fish stock if you wish to achieve a more intense flavour; in quantity, barely enough to cover the slices; then it should be boiled on a high heat for just a few minutes. Additions may be made, such as seafood, diced potatoes, crushed almonds and parsley, paprika etc., additions which lend diver-

sity and richness to this maritime cuisine, the most elaborate presentations of which, featuring various species of fish, accompanied by molluscs and crustaceans, receive such flamboyant names as *zarzuelas* (operettas) or *óperas*.

The small fish, those which have no place in the casserole, are earmarked for the frying pan, that is, they too are immersed in boiling oil. As the saying by the sage **Archaestratus** goes: «small fish should just be shown the heat». The shore dwellers of the Mare Nostrum learned this lesson well, and for centuries it has been on these coasts where fish has been fried best; because the latter only feels the effect of the heat when the oil has reached the optimum temperature to achieve a light,

golden crust which prevents the fried fish from becoming too dry. And lastly, remember that it is on these beaches where the seafood, either grilled (an invention of the Levante region, i.e. Valencia, Castellón, Alicante and Murcia), or in small casseroles, with garlic and chilli, and naturally the bubbling oil, reaches its maximum gastronomic peaks.

The third element of the abovementioned trilogy are the rice dishes. Existing throughout Mediterranean Spain, they are gradually encroaching ever further inland. Rice cookery also has as its base, in almost all its culinary processes, the *sofrito*. You may use the cooking pot, the casserole or the frying pan, but you will always begin the operation by making a *sofrito* in oil with vegetables, meat, fish, and seafood. Rice is of an amiable nature and it accepts all kinds of company. Once the *sofrito* is made, the stock is added, often only water, and then the rice, which is sometimes previously lightly fried, according to the culinary variation, and finally the dish is boiled. Rice dishes, according to the container in which they are cooked, will turn out *runny* if one opts for the pot, *sticky* if you choose a saucepan or concave casserole dish; *dry*, if you prefer a flat baking dish, frying pan or *paella* dish. There are thus three techniques, depending on the aforementioned container, but, given that there is hardly any ingredient which cannot lend its support and

In Spain, bovine, ovine and porcine livestock supply the meats which are habitually consumed, but when one speaks simply of the roast, it is always understood that one is making reference to roast lamb.

its flavour to the rice, there are countless variations. There are those which boast a long tradition; people have become accustomed to them throughout the years, and consider them classic; but human ingenuity is infinite, cooks invent, conceive other combinations of flavouring elements, new rice dishes emerge continually, some last and others are soon forgotten.

A simple way of cooking? Its simplicity is only apparent; especially in the dry rice dishes, the best results are only obtained after a lot of practice; achieving a good paella always entails a certain amount of risk, as there are many factors which must be taken into account: the quality of the ingredients, the nature of the water, the intensity of the heat, not to mention carelessness or error. Indeed, the success of a paella lies in its very difficulty. There are thousands, perhaps millions of Spaniards who like to boast that they are masters in the complex art of preparing a paella, and they never waste an opportunity to prove it to their relatives and friends.

The paella is of unknown and modest origins, no-one knows in which farmhouse or cottage of the fertile region of Valencia it was born; undoubtedly, as a special dish for a festive day, as a preparation which had to be cooked in the open air on the occasion of a merry country outing, and not as an example of home cooking; but the number of its followers gra-

dually grew. First the farmworkers were its regular consumers, then the inhabitants of the cities discovered it and took a liking to it when they visited their country residences. The second step was when the paella arrived at the restaurants; first of all, it appeared in the more modest eating houses on the coast, subsequently extending to the «posher» establishments of Alicante and Valencia, where the ingredients which had always been considered a luxury were added to the rice, such as lobster. In the forties, the paella had reached every city in Spain, and consequently other regional variations emerged. Package tourism arrived and the paella, with its multicoloured beauty, dazzled the travellers, who on returning to their countries of origin became its best heralds. Today the paella is the figurehead of Spanish cuisine throughout the world.

ATLANTIC SPAIN

In Atlantic Spain we also have a gastronomic trilogy, namely that of stews, roasts and large fish. The cooking pot is probably the oldest vessel invented by Man, and for this reason its remains are found at all archaeological excavation sites. As a result of its being used to cook vegetables, pulses and meat, a culinary preparation was created which takes its name from that of the container, and which therefore has taken the name of *olla* (pot), or even *puchero or pote*, and which

is common to all the Western regions. The *olla podrida* (it should be taken into account that *podrida* used to mean powerful, that is to say rich in ingredients, and not the current meaning of "rotten"!) was the great dish of Spain's cuisine in those glorious times in which in her dominions the sun never set, and the *olla podrida* reached the courts of the whole of Europe, as it was taken there by the cooks of our ambassadors.

Although it has lost part of its splendour (in the version of **Diego Granados**, chef of **Phillip IV**, it contained fifty two ingredients), this dish has spawned worthy and honourable descendants to be found all over the country. So many were to arise that, on a certain occasion, recipes of as many as ninety six different versions were put together, in which the most diverse ingredients were employed. And among so many formulas were the *berza malagueña*; the *pote gallego*; the *escudella i carn d'olla* from Cataluña; the *puchero* from Valencia; that of the seven meats from the Canaries, and so on until we complete the eight dozen mentioned above. And, although the choice is difficult, in this recipe book preference has been given to the Castilian version, to the traditional *cocido madrileño* (chick-pea stew), since not in vain Madrid is the capital of the kingdom.

The second place in this culinary trinity belongs to the roast. In Spain, bovine, ovine and porcine livestock supply the meats which are habitually consumed, but when one speaks simply of a roast, it is always understood that one is making reference to roast lamb. The roast has also undergone some changes throughout the centuries. Thus, in the period of the **Hapsburgs**, it was roasted on a spit; in many a mansion, the swords of Toledo steel which had been brandished in battles and duels ended up relegated to the kitchens and were used to skewer the kid goats, suckling pigs and poultry. Subsequently, the casserole roast has come to triumph, and in Spain, in dozens of cities, hundreds of inn-style restaurants compete in the sumptuous preparation of roast lamb and suckling pig.

Moreover, Spanish cooks have known how to make good culinary use of the entrails of the meat, even the least noble parts, and therefore, amongst our tastiest dishes are *kidneys in sherry*; *sweetbreads* prepared in a hundred different ways and *rabo de toro* or bull's tail, a dish so intimately linked to the bullfight.

The trinity is completed by the large fish. Those of the Atlantic and the Bay of Biscay, even when they belong to the same species, are greater in size than their Mediterranean counterparts. They are therefore cooked in a different way, being prevalent the roasting of whole pieces, displayed in all their splendour, either charcoal-grilled or in the oven, which allows the cook to increase their gastronomic appeal by means of suitable fillings, garnishes and sauces.

Bream, sea bass, hake, turbot, these are the stars of Galician, Cantabrian and Basque cuisine. As the saying here goes, «*El asador nace, el cocinero se hace*» (Whereas a cook can learn his trade, one hast to be born a roaster). This is a compliment which highlights the difficulty of mastering this part of culinary science; if it is difficult to roast meat, it is even more so with fish, due to its delicateness. A baked bream which retains its juicy texture can be a sublime delicacy and, on the other hand, a slight oversight in its cooking can turn it into a dry, crumbly, inedible disaster. The recipes for these dishes indicate the path to follow, but with these more than with any others, those who attempt them should take special care.

Cod deserves a special mention; it has been stated that in the field of gastronomy, salted cod is rather like the resurrection of the flesh, and there is a lot of truth in this statement, provided, logically, that the cod is treated by expert hands. Because it is a genuine resurrection, starting off with a dry, salted product and turning it into juicy, delicious and succulent culinary preparations. These objectives are not attained without knowing the material in depth, without mastering the technique; indeed, there are many cooks or housewives who jealously guard their own special secrets, to achieve an average cod is relatively easy, but to go one step further, and arrive at an optimum result, is not within everyone's reach. There are many recipes for cooking cod, a lot can be said about it and much has been written, but Spain, among many others, guards three gems: *ajoarriero*, Biscay style (*a la vizcaína*) and *pil-pil*; in what is a true expression of the difficulty of preparing such cod dishes, it has been said that one of their essential ingredients is the sweat of the cook as he gently cradles the casserole containing his creation.

An addition should be made to this trilogy of Atlantic Spain, to include one of the uses to which vegetables are put. In the basin of one of the rivers which flow into the Ocean, the Guadalquivir, we find one of the most original preparations of Spanish cuisine: *gazpacho*. The latter, with all its local variations, although it was born of popular wisdom, appears to have been conceived by the most experienced nutrition experts, as it is not only refreshing, but also perfectly balanced with regard to calories and vitamins, and most suitable for the hot Andalusian summer.

NATIONAL INSTITUTIONS

The cuisines of Mediterranean and Atlantic Spain are interwoven and linked, they amicably lend or transfer to each other their best culinary accomplishments; but there are also dishes or speciali-

The cuisines of Mediterranean and Atlantic Spain are interwoven and linked, they amicably lend or transfer to each other their best culinary accomplishments.

ties accepted and admired by everyone, as some of them are genuine *national insitutions*, which no Spanish city or town can claim as their exclusive property.

Among these is the potato omelette, Spanish omelette (*tortilla de patatas* or *española*), a marvel to all who come to know it. Long before **Parmentier** made the potato known in France, and its cultivation then spread throughout Europe, it had already arrived in Spain, and no-one knows in which undiscovered corner this amiable pact between the American tuber, the egg and olive oil was made. Modest, simple, but like everything in cookery classified as simple, difficult, since it requires a perfect balance between its three components; the Spa-

nish omelette is like a minor star, but at the same time a resplendent sun which shines on the Spaniards during their country outings, their picnics on the beach, their receptions and cocktail parties, and never lets them down.

Some of these national institutions are early risers, they comfort the Spaniard first thing in the morning, such as *churros* - another of the virtues of olive oil! Many others, as you will discover by reading these pages, appear at the beginning or in the middle of lunches and dinners, and others are reserved for dessert. It is not surprising that Spanish confectionery is so extensive and varied, if one recalls that sugar entered Europe, like so many other products, through Spain, where the

cultivation of the sugar cane was customary and still exists in the fertile plains of Granada. Rice pudding, sponge cakes, swiss rolls (known as «gypsy's arms» or *brazos de gitano*), fried milk, compotes, custard and French toast bear witness to this gastronomic galaxy of so many different varieties of pastries, sweets and cakes; as there is not one single city, not one single village in the whole extension of the Iberian Peninsula, which does not have its own confectionery.

Counting the grains of sand on the beach or counting the stars in the heavens are hackneyed phrases to highlight the difficulty of exhaustively enumerating a series of singular things, and both clichés are applicable when it comes to the task of compiling a list of Spanish gastronomic specialities. We have attempted to choose from among the most outstanding, from among the most famous, but a selection, whichever criterion is followed, must always leave out hundreds of others of similar merits. Nevertheless, the recipes contained in this publication are sufficiently representative example of Spain's cuisine. A cuisine which does not have to compete with any other, which does not need to be acclaimed as the best in the world; it is satisfied with being that of the nation which has created it.

Lorenzo Millo

Black olives

Aceitunas negras

Ingredients for 4 servings:

1/4 kg (1/2 lb) black olives
1/2 chopped onion
2 tablespoons olive oil
1 teaspoon hot paprika
1 squeeze lemon juice

Easy

- Preparation time:
  5 minutes.

1. Place the olives in a bowl and add the rest of the raw ingredients on top. Stir well and leave to stand.

Suggestion

If the olives are green you can add gherkins.

Elvers

Angulas

Ingredients for 4 servings:

1/4 kg (1/2 lb) elvers
2 tablespoons olive oil
2 cloves garlic
Salt

Easy

- Preparation time:
  10 minutes.

1. Choose large white elvers, rejecting the thin dark ones. Wash thoroughly.

2. Heat the water in a saucepan with the salt; when it comes to the boil, add the elvers and leave to boil for one minute. Drain and dry with a cloth.

3. Fry the garlic in olive oil in a heat-resistant earthenware dish. Add the elvers and heat without frying.

4. Serve immediately, either in the same dish or in individual dishes.

Squid rings in batter

Calamares a la romana

Ingredients for 4 servings:

1/2 kg (1 lb) squid
Flour
Salt
Bicarbonate of soda

Easy

- Preparation time:
  30 minutes.

1. Wash and throughly clean the squid and cut into strips or rings.

2. Make a batter to coat them using water, flour, salt and a little bicarbonate of soda to make it light.

3. Coat the squid in this batter and fry in abundant boiling oil.

Potatoes in garlic mayonnaise

Patatas al alioli

Ingredients:

2 large potatoes
2 cloves garlic
1 1/2 cups olive oil
Salt
Chopped parsley

Quick

- Preparation time:
  30 minutes.

1. Peel the potatoes, wash thoroughly and place in a saucepan covered in water and salt; boil until soft (approximately 15 minutes) but not crumbling. Drain and leave to cool.

2. Whilst the potatoes are boiling, place the peeled garlic in a mortar with the salt, crush well, and when it forms a paste, add the oil gradually in a thin trickle whilst continuing to stir in order to bind the sauce.

3. Slice the potatoes and place in a bowl. Cover with the garlic and oil sauce and sprinkle with the chopped parsley.

Photo: Squid rings in batter

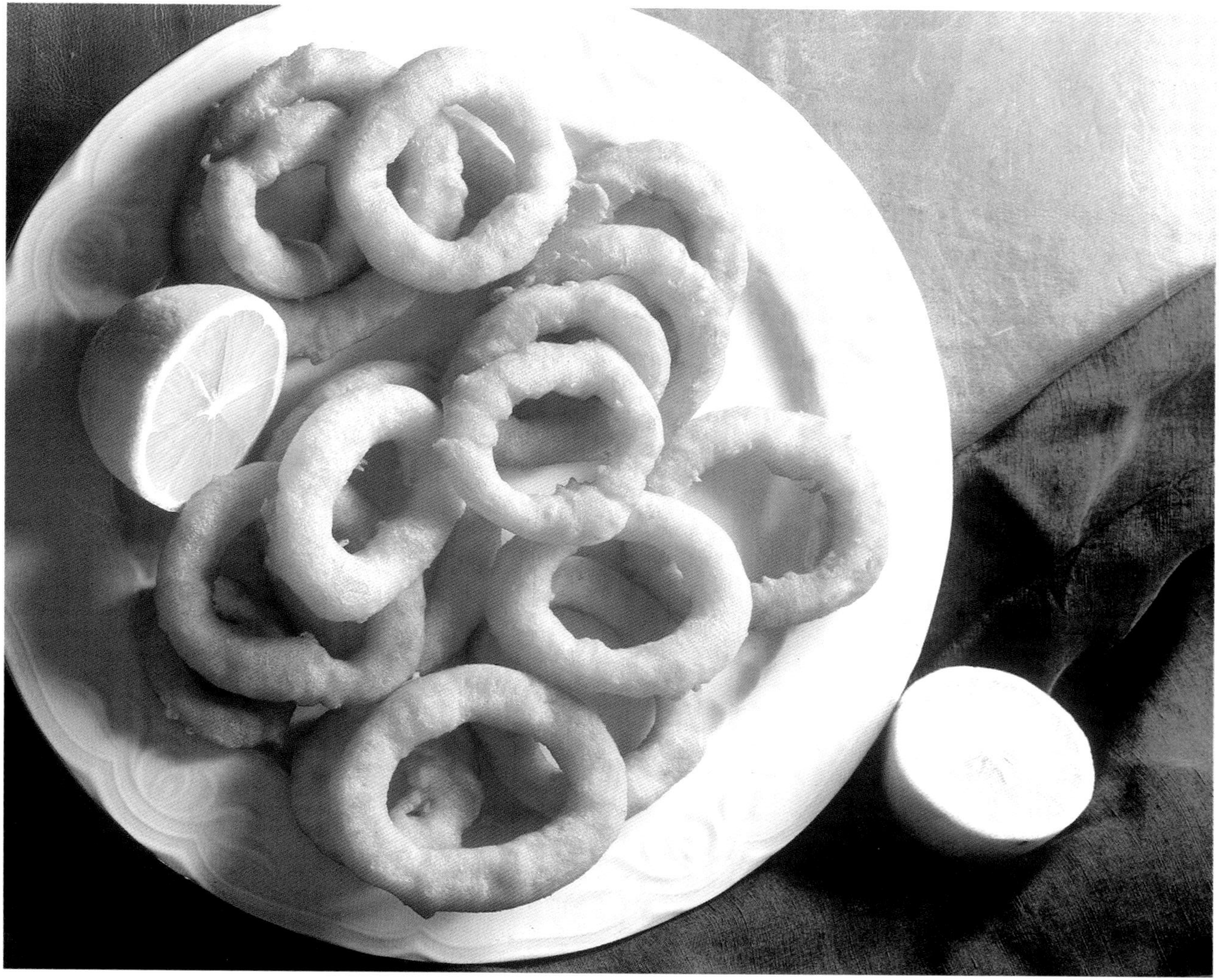

HORS D'OEUVRES AND SAUCES

Chorizo (seasoned pork sausage) in cider

Chorizo a la sidra

Ingredients:
250 g (1/2 lb) homemade chorizo
1/2 litre (1 pint) cider

Quick
Easy

• Preparation time:
25 minutes

1. Lightly wash and dry the chorizos. Place the chorizos in a pre-heated saucepan, pour on the cider, cover and cook for 15 to 20 minutes.
2. Remove the chorizos and place them on a wooden board, slice and place in small earthenware dishes with the cider which is left after cooking.
3. Serve hot.

Prawns in garlic sauce

Gambas al ajillo

Ingredients for 4 servings:
1/2 kg (1 lb) prawns
4 cloves garlic
Chilli
Olive oil

Easy

• Preparation time:
30 minutes.

1. Peel the prawns and place in salted water for a few minutes.
2. Place the peeled prawn tails in individual earthenware dishes and sprinkle over them the chopped garlic and chilli according to taste.
3. Cover with boiling oil and leave for a few minutes on the hob or burner.
4. Remove and serve immediately whilst boiling, placing the dishes on a small plate to avoid burning oneself.

Prawns in batter

Gambas a la gabardina

Ingredients for 4 servings:
1/2 kg (1 lb) prawns
2 eggs
3 tablespoons milk
Salt, flour
Olive oil

Easy

• Preparation time:
30 minutes.

1. Boil the peeled prawn tails in salted water for two minutes.
2. Prepare a batter in the following way: beat two egg whites until stiff, gradually add the milk, a pinch of salt and the necessary flour to make a thick batter.
3. Coat the prawns in this batter, picking them up by their tails, and fry in abundant hot oil.
4. Serve hot.

Suggestion

They may be coated in the same batter as used for «Squid rings in batter» and also with a paste made from half a small coffee cup of milk, the same measure of soda water and flour.

Pasties

Empanadillas

Ingredients for 4 servings:

For the pastry:

1/2 glass white wine

1/2 glass water

1/2 glass olive oil

Salt

1/2 tablespoon baking powder

Flour (as much as required)

For the filling:

Meat, fish, tuna or boiled eggs, all previously prepared and finely-chopped

Easy

- Preparation time:
  40 minutes.

1. Mix the wine, oil and water. Dissolve in this mixture the salt and baking powder and gradually add the necessary flour to form a paste, not very stiff, which is left to stand for half an hour.

2. At the end of this time, roll out and cut into circles with a glass; place in each of them a teaspoon of the mixture prepared for the filling.

3. Close the pasty and press the edges with your fingertips or a fork to keep the filling in.

4. Fry in abundant hot oil, pouring the latter on top with a skimmer to avoid having to turn them over.

Suggestion

The pastry can be made with milk instead of water and wine, or by adding a beaten egg; the pastry cases can also be bought ready made. The filling may also be a sweet cream.

HORS D'OEUVRES AND SAUCES

Croquettes

Croquetas

Ingredients for 4 servings:
Olive oil
1/2 l (1 pint) milk
4 tablespoons flour
Salt
Minced meat, cured ham, or fish, etc.
Breadcrumbs
2 eggs

Complicated

* Preparation time:
  40 minutes.

1. In the oil, in which you have previously fried garlic, bread, orange peel, etc., lightly fry the flour until slightly golden. Gradually add the cold milk, stirring continuously for around 15 minutes until it boils. This paste should be thicker than normal white sauce.
2. The mince is lightly fried in the frying pan and added to the cooked paste.
3. Spread the whole mixture over a dish dampened with cool water and leave to cool.
4. Beat two eggs and place the breadcrumbs on another plate.
5. Once the paste is cool, take a portion of the same to make a croquette, shape it, dip it in the egg, then in the breadcrumbs and fry in very hot, abundant oil.

Suggestion

To make the paste, the milk can be replaced with meat stock. They can also be made just with the cream.

White sauce

Salsa blanca (bechamel)

Ingredients:
1/2 l (1 pint) milk
2 or 3 tablespoons flour
1 tablespoon butter or 2 of olive oil
Salt

Easy

* Preparation time:
  15 minutes.

1. Mix the flour to a paste with the cold milk. Add the butter or oil and cook for 10-12 minutes, stirring well to prevent it from sticking.
2. Once cooked, add the salt and stir to give it consistency.

Alternative version:

It can also be made by lightly frying the flour in the hot oil or butter (2 tablespoons of oil for one of flour), gradually adding the milk until the desired thickness is attained, stirring well to remove the lumps.

Mayonnaise

Mahonesa

Ingredients:
1 egg
1 tablespoon vinegar or lemon juice
1/4 l (1/2 pint) olive oil
Salt

Easy

* Preparation time:
  2 minutes.

1. Place in the bowl of the blender, in this order, the egg, vinegar, salt and oil.
2. Lower the arm of the blender right to the bottom; turn it on and do not move until all the oil binds.
3. Without stopping the blender, raise slowly until it almost reaches the top of the mayonnaise, then rapidly lower it once or twice and the mayonnaise will be ready.

Note

This recipe is intended for use with a blender. However, the mayonnaise can also be made be hand. In this case the oil must be added gradually.

Upper photo: Croquettes
Lower photo: White sauce

Fish sauce

Salsa de pescado

Ingredients:

1/2 kg (1 lb) fish heads, bones, tails and fins
1 small glass of white wine
3 leeks
1/4 kg (1/2 lb) tomatoes
3 tablespoons butter
Juice of half a lemon
Parsley
Salt
Pepper
1 tablespoon flour
Oil

Easy

• Preparation time:
  30 minutes.

1. Wash the fish heads, bones, tails and fins thoroughly and boil in water.
2. Lightly fry a tablespoon of flour in the butter; then add the chopped leek, a little pepper and the white wine and cook for a few minutes.
3. Add the sliced tomatoes, without pips, the chopped parsley and the lemon juice. Cook for a few minutes longer.
4. Strain the fish stock and add to the above mixture. Cook until it reaches the desired thickness.
5. Strain again and serve hot.

Garlic mayonnaise

Alioli

Ingredients:

Sauce mayonnaise
2 cloves garlic

Easy

• Preparation time:
  5 minutes.

1. Once the mayonnaise is prepared (see recipe) add the garlic (crushed to a pulp) according to taste. Stir well.

Photo: Garlic mayonnaise

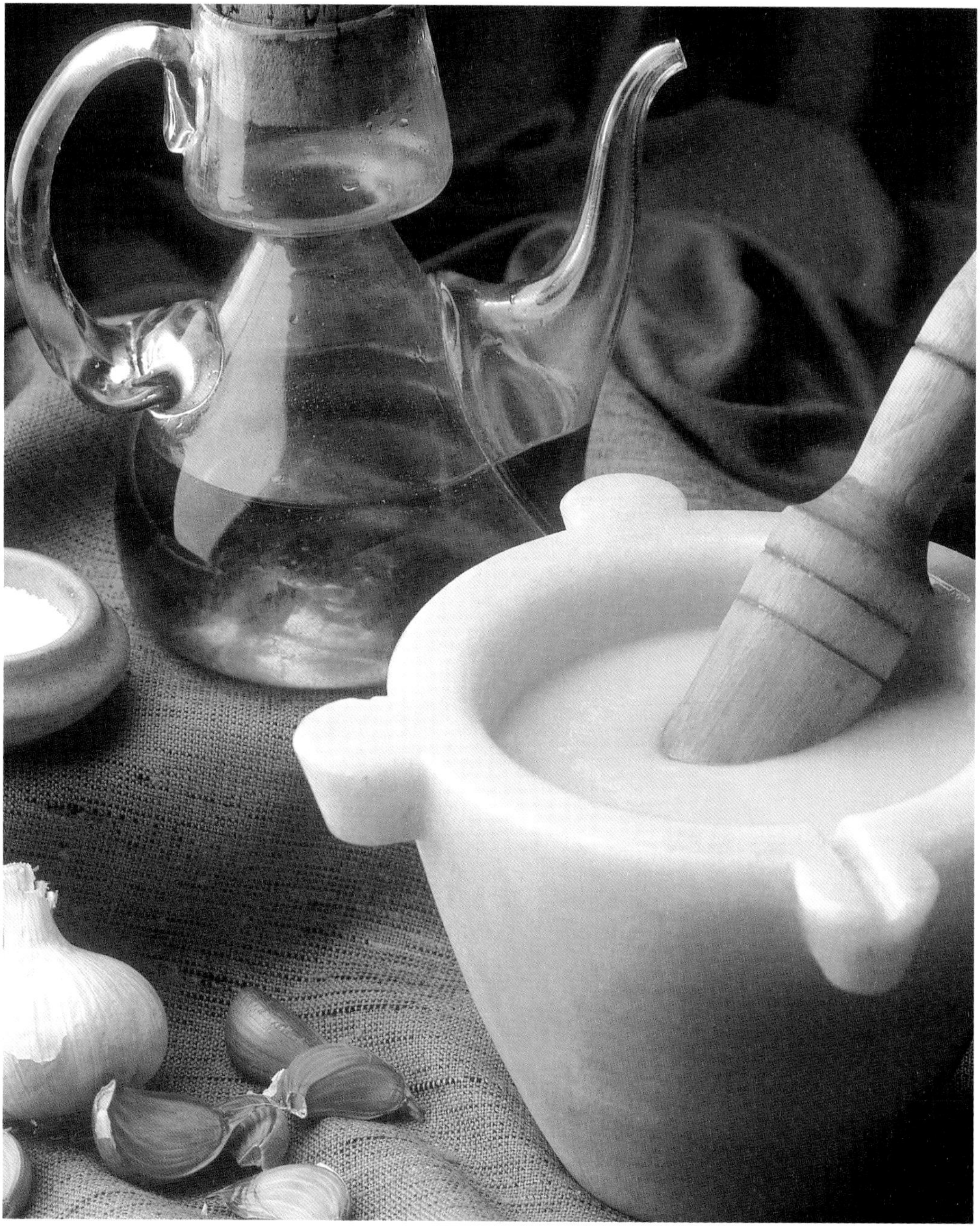

HORS D'OEUVRES AND SAUCES

Sauce for everything

Salsa para todo

Ingredients:

2 coffee cups meat stock

3 large lemons

1 1/2 cups white wine

1 clove

Pepper

Salt

1 piece of orange peel

Bay leaf

Easy

• Preparation time:
  2 minutes.

1. Place all the ingredients into an earthenware or glass casserole dish. Cover well and leave in a cool place for approximately ten hours.
2. At the end of this time, pour into a bottle and keep to use when needed. It keeps for a long time.

Garlic sauce

Salsa al ajoarriero

Ingredients:

Garlic

Lemon

Oil

Salt

Easy

• Preparation time:
  5 minutes.

1. Crush the garlic in a mortar. Add a squeeze of lemon juice and a reasonable amount of oil. Season with salt and stir well.

Parsley sauce

Salsa verde

Ingredients:

2 tablespoons flour

Olive oil

1 teaspoon finely chopped onion

Parsley, salt

Garlic

Stock or water

Easy

• Preparation time:
  5 minutes.

1. In hot oil lightly fry the flour and the onion (finely chopped and then crushed in a mortar) until golden.

2. Once golden, add the stock or water (approximately a quarter of a litre) and cook for a few minutes; season with salt.
3. Crush a few parsley leaves in the mortar. Mix with a little water and add to the sauce when it is cooked. This sauce is suitable for accompanying pulses and fish.

Vinaigrette

Salsa vinagreta

Ingredients:

Garlic

Lemon

Onion

Parsley

Olive oil

Salt

Easy

• Preparation time:
  5 minutes.

1. Finely chop the onion, parsley and garlic. Add refined oil and a squeeze of lemon. Season with salt mixed with a little water. Stir well until it acquires the desired thickness. Serve with salads and boiled fish.

Photo: Vinaigrette

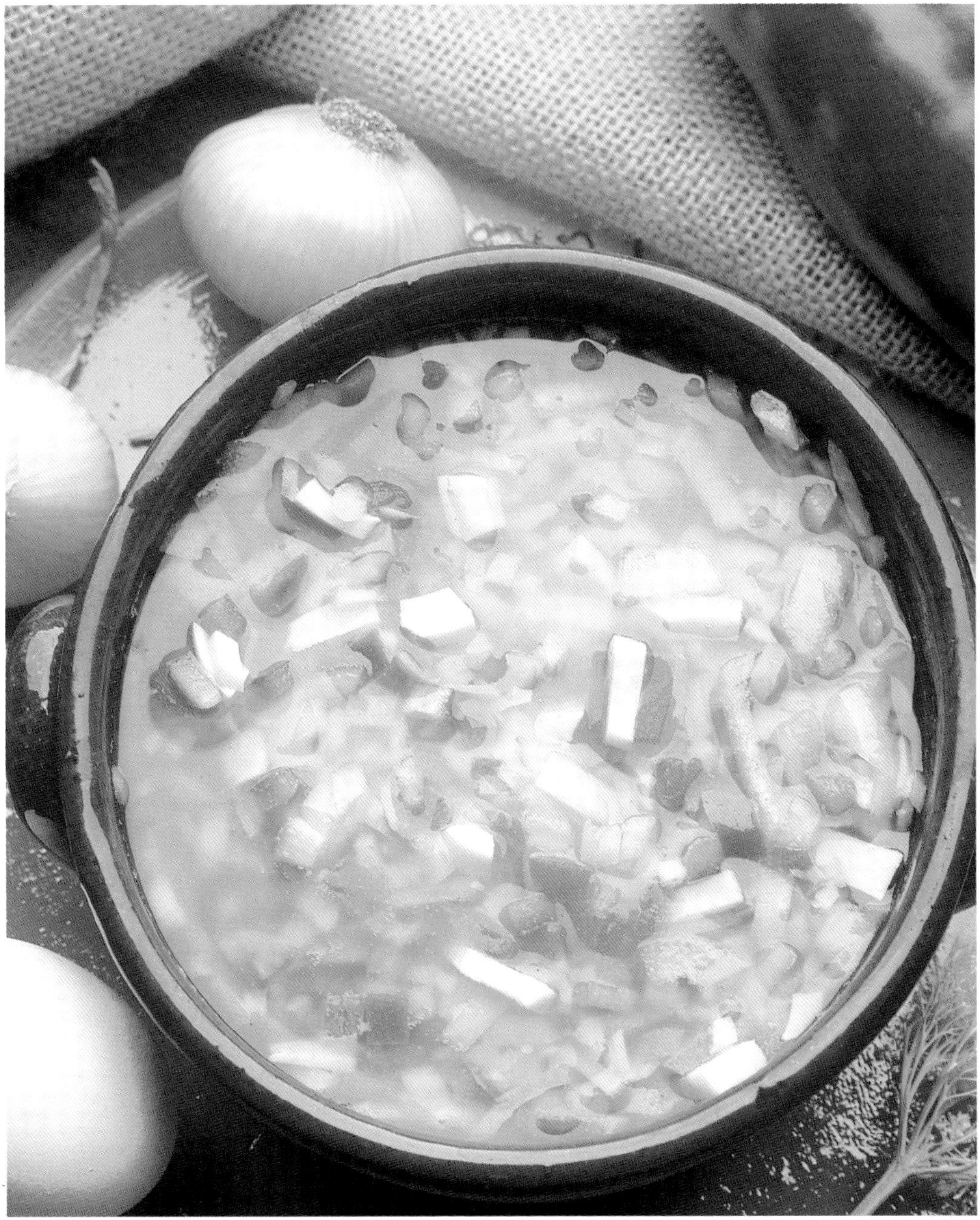

Vegetable salad

Ensalada de verduras

Ingredients for 4 servings:
1/2 kg (1 lb) artichokes
200 g (7 oz) peas
3 carrots
6 asparagus
2 medium potatoes
Lemon juice
White pepper
Mustard
Chilli
Olive oil
Salt

Easy

- Preparation time:
  30 minutes.

1. Boil all the vegetables, except the asparagus, in salted water. Cut into equal pieces and strain.
2. Make a sauce with lemon juice, oil, salt and the spices, according to taste; mix well and pour over the cooked vegetables.
3. Mix well and decorate with the asparagus, also seasoned with the sauce.

Russian salad

Ensaladilla rusa

Ingredients for 4 servings:
1/4 kg (1/2 lb) green beans
1/4 kg (1/2 lb) unpeeled potatoes
100 g (3 1/2 oz) peas
100 g (3 1/2 oz) gherkins
Mayonnaise

Easy

- Preparation time:
  40 minutes.

1. Wash the potatoes, without peeling, and boil them whole. Also boil the green beans.
2. Once cooked, peel the potatoes and cut into small pieces. Likewise, slice the beans.
3. Mix the potatoes and beans with the peas, gherkins and olives, also sliced.
4. Mix together and add the mayonnaise (see recipe).

Tomato salad

Ensalada de tomate

Ingredients:
Top quality tomatoes
Hard boiled eggs
Mayonnaise
Lettuce
Onion
Lemon
Olive oil
Salt
Garlic

Easy

- Preparation time:
  20 minutes.

1. Slice the tomatoes, sprinkle with salt and cover with a mixture of three parts oil to one of lemon juice, well stirred.
2. Cut the boiled eggs in half and remove the yolk; mix the latter with mayonnaise (see recipe) and refill the eggs with this paste. Place on top of the tomatoes with the convex part upwards.
3. Wash and slice the lettuce and onion; add a dressing of lemon, oil, salt and garlic. Use to fill the empty spaces between the tomatoes.

Photo: Vegetable salad

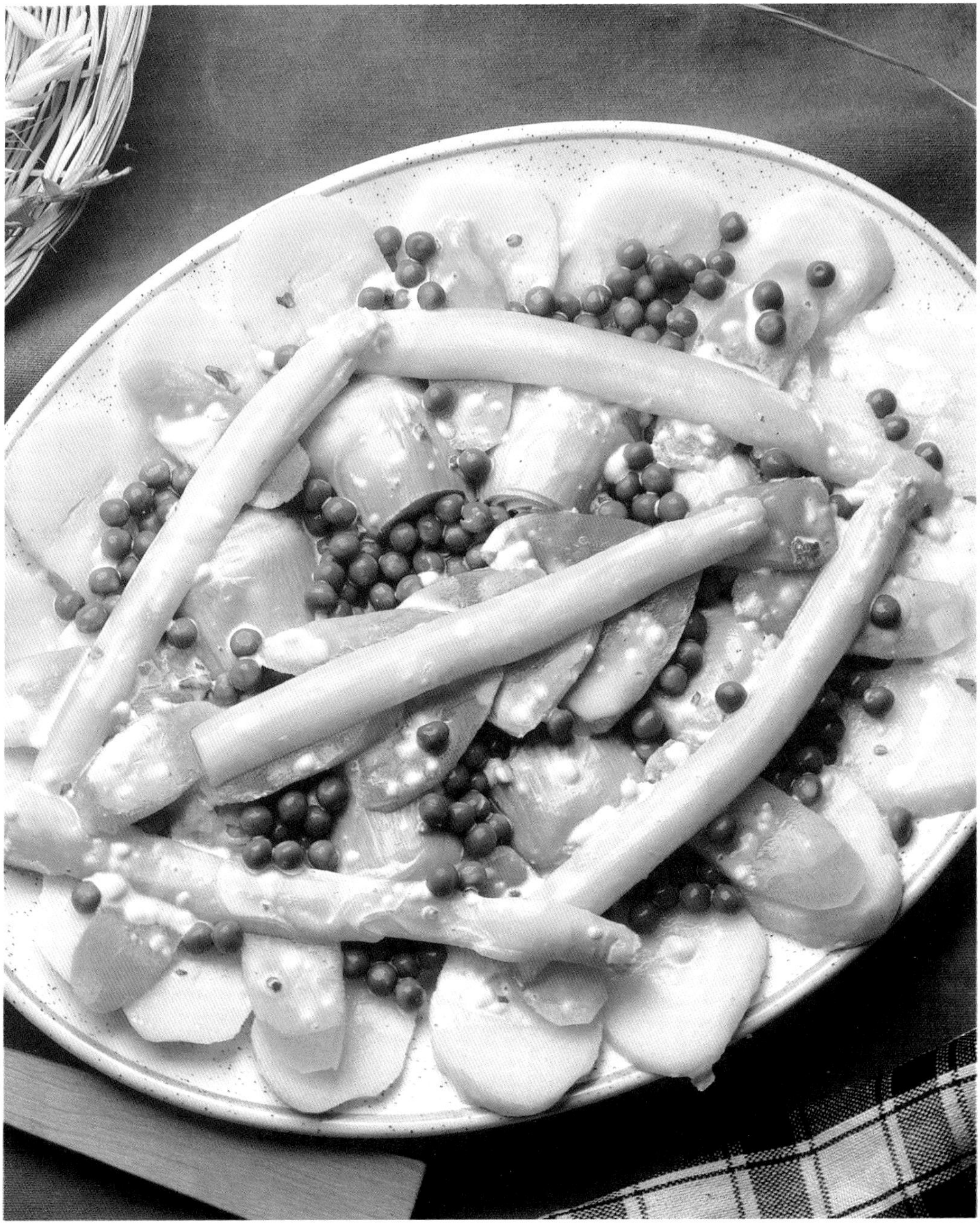

Stuffed aubergines

Berenjenas rellenas

Ingredients for 4 servings:
8 small aubergines
1 egg
100 g (3 1/2 oz) hazelnuts and pine kernels
200 g (7 oz) minced meat
50 g (1 3/4 oz) cured ham
1 cup stock or water
Olive oil
Salt
1/2 onion
1 clove garlic
1/2 tablespoon grated cheese
1 tablespoon butter

Complicated

- Preparation time: 1 hour.

1. Wash the aubergines thoroughly and cut into two lengthways. Soak in salted water for half an hour.
2. Strain and remove the pulp, which is placed on one side.
3. In the oil, lightly fry 3/4 of the onion, the garlic, mince, ham and the pulp of the aubergine. Season with salt.
4. Fry the rest of the onion separately, add the crushed hazelnuts and pine kernels and the stock without salt. Cook for approximately 20 minutes.
5. Strain the stock prepared earlier and pour over the aubergines.
6. Place in the oven again and bake for 30 minutes, sprinkled with grated cheese. They should turn out succulent but without too much sauce.

Meat and vegetable pie

Budín de verduras y carne

Ingredients for 4 servings:

200 g (7 oz) meat

Onion

1 clove garlic

Cabbage

Parsley, salt, olive oil

Stock or water

White sauce

Breadcrumbs

Complicated

• Preparation time:
  40 minutes.

1. Wash and slice the cabbage. Boil in water or stock until soft.
2. Lightly fry the meat in a frying pan with a little oil until golden. Add the onion, garlic and parsley, all finely chopped. Tomatoes or peppers may also be added. Season with salt.
3. Once the cabbage is cooked, strain well and mix with the lightly fried meat.
4. Grease a mould with butter or oil and sprinkle it with breadcrumbs. Place in it the cabbage and meat mixture, stir well.
5. Turn out the mould onto a suitable dish and cover with very hot white sauce (see recipe). Serve immediately.

Note

Curly or Galician cabbage is richer in vitamins and minerals than white cabbage.

Cauliflower salad

Coliflor en ensalada

Ingredients for 4 servings:

1 large cauliflower

Olive oil

Paprika

Lemon juice

Salt

1 clove garlic

Easy

• Preparation time:
  15 minutes.

1. Wash the cauliflower and cut into pieces. Boil in salted water.
2. Fry a clove of garlic in oil until golden; remove the frying pan from the heat and add a little paprika and a dash of lemon.
3. Strain the cauliflower and place in a dish. Pour over it the previously prepared sauce and stir to soak it well.

Peas with cured ham

Guisantes con jamón

Ingredients for 4 servings:

1/2 kg (1 lb) peas
1/4 kg (1/2 lb) cured ham with a little fat
Butter or olive oil
1 onion
Parsley
Lettuce hearts
1 glass stock or water
Salt
1 clove garlic
Croutons

Easy

- Preparation time: 30 minutes.

1. Melt the butter in a frying pan, or heat the oil. Lightly fry the ham, which has been cut into squares, for a few moments.
2. Immediately add the peas, then the onion and parsley in large pieces, plus the lettuce hearts and the whole clove of garlic. Season with salt, taking into account the flavour of the ham.
3. Once all this is fried, add the stock or water and cook until the peas are tender.
4. Serve with or without sauce, surrounded by croutons.

Stuffed peppers

Pimientos rellenos

Ingredients for 4 servings:

8 small peppers
300 g (10 1/2 oz) minced meat or ham
1 onion
1 clove garlic
Parsley
1 or 2 eggs
Breadcrumbs
Olive oil
Salt
2 medium tomatoes
Stock or water

Complicated

- Preparation time: 40 minutes.

1. Wash the peppers and remove the stalks. Through this hole, remove the seeds inside, taking care not to break them. Wash the inside and drain the water.
2. Prepare a filling with the peeled, seedless tomatoes, a slice of onion, garlic and a sprig of parsley, all finely chopped, and add to this the meat seasoned with salt.
3. Bind the above mixture with beaten egg and fill the peppers by placing them face upwards. Fry.
4. Once fried, place in a saucepan, cover with stock and boil until soft.

5. Once boiled, peel carefully and place on a serving dish. Sieve the stock used in boiling and pour over the peppers.

Ratatouille

Pisto

Ingredients for 4 servings:

1/4 kg (1/2 lb) potatoes
1 tomato
1 pepper
1 clove garlic
Parsley
Olive oil
Salt
2 eggs
1 large slice of ham with fat

Easy

- Preparation time: 40 minutes.

1. Peel and wash the potatoes; cut into squares, salt and fry.
2. Add to the potatoes the ham, cut into squares, the chopped onion, the garlic and the pepper. When it is all well fried, add the tomato, peeled and seedless, and the two beaten eggs.
3. Season with salt and stir well. Serve immediately once the eggs are done.

Photo: Ratatouille

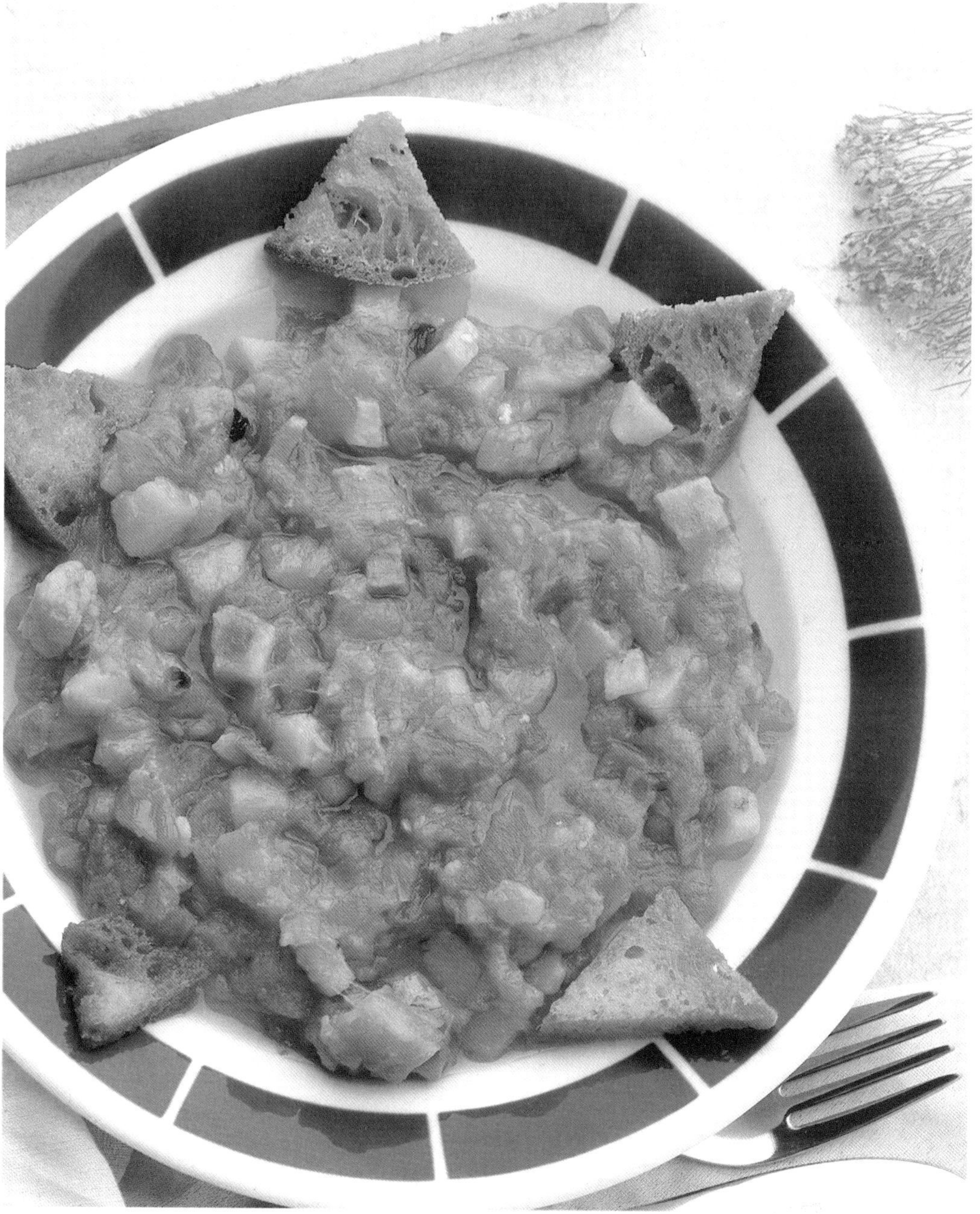

Meat stock

Caldo de carne

Ingredients:

2 small carrots

1 leek

1/4 kg (1/2 lb) beef

2 or 3 kg (4 to 6 lbs) bones

1 clove garlic

Sprigs of parsley

Salt

Easy

• Preparation time:
  1 hour.

1. Boil the leek, onion, parsley, garlic (unpeeled but clean), carrots, bones and meat in sufficient water to cover all the ingredients.

2. Cook with the lid on until the liquid is reduced to a approximately a bowlful.

3. Leave to cool, remove the fat and season with salt. Keep in a cool place.

4. When you need meat stock, mix a tablespoon of the above preparation with half a litre of hot or boiling water.
If you want a sauce, use less water.

Chicken consommé

Caldo de gallina

Ingredients:

1/4 kg (1/2 lb) chicken

1 small coffee cup chick-peas

1 beef bone, preferably a knuckle.

1 sprig parsley, 1 clove garlic

Onion, 2 small carrots

Salt, 1 piece cured ham

Easy

• Preparation time:
  3 hours.

1. In two litres (4 pints) of cold water, place the chicken, cleaned and passed over a flame to remove the remains of the feathers, the ham and the rest of the ingredients except the salt. Simmer in a normal pot for around three hours. Season with salt.

2. Once boiled, strain and serve, either plain or with the addition of slices of bread, a broken egg yolk, or making a soup (with noodles etc).

Note

If it is made in a pressure cooker, use only a litre and a half (3 pints) of water. In this case the cooking time is reduced to around 20 minutes.

Galician soup

Caldo gallego

Ingredients for 4 servings:

1 ham (foreleg)
150 g (5 oz) salted rib or backbone
100 g (3 1/2 oz) bacon
1 bowlful dried beans
6 whole potatoes (average sized)
6 large cabbage leaves
1 tablespoon lard
1 chorizo (seasoned pork sausage)
Paprika

Easy

* Preparation time:
  45 minutes.

1. The beans should be soaked for several hours, for example overnight.
2. Boil all the ingredients except the bacon, lard and salt in two litres of water, taking into account that the potatoes should be peeled but whole.
3. When it is all cooked -it takes approximately half an hour- melt the lard in a frying pan, lightly fry the paprika and pour into the soup.
If you put in chorizo, you may leave out the paprika. Season with salt and leave to stand for a few minutes before serving.

Suggestion

If you use a pressure cooker to make this dish, it will take only around 10 minutes.

Gazpacho (Cold soup)

Ingredients for 4 servings:

6 medium tomatoes
2 Spring onions
3 cucumbers
2 glasses water
Salt
Pepper
Slices of bread
Garlic
Parsley
Lemon

Easy

- Preparation time:
  5 minutes.

1. Finely chop all the ingredients.
2. Prepare a mixture with a squeeze of lemon, oil and salt. Cover all the ingredients with this dressing. Add the water and stir well.

Suggestion

It may be served with an ice cube in each bowl.

Castillian chick-pea stew

Cocido castellano

Ingredients for 4 servings:

4 handfuls chick-peas
200 g (7 oz) cured meat or ham
1 piece longaniza or chorizo (seasoned pork sausages)
100 g (3 1/2 oz) 3rd class beef
100 g (3 1/2 oz) pork fat
1 bone
1 Spring onion or 1 leek
Noodles
Cabbage
Olive oil
Lemon
Salt

Complicated

- Preparation time:
  1 hour.

1. Soak the chick-peas in hot water for 8 to 10 hours.
2. Boil the chick-peas with all the meat; when everything is almost cooked, season with salt.
3. In a separate saucepan (or in the pan that comes with the pot), boil the vegetables with pieces of onion and garlic.
4. Once the vegetables are cooked, add salt and pour over them hot oil in which a little paprika has been lightly fried.
5. Pour part of the stock from boiling the chick-peas into another saucepan and boil the noodles in it for 10 minutes.
6. There are various ways of serving this dish: generally the soup is served first and then the chick-peas accompanied by the meat and vegetables.

Suggestion

The boiled vegetables may be replaced by a raw lettuce and tomato salad. One type of meat may be replaced by meat of another kind; chicken is especially good.

Photo: Castillian chick-pea stew

Rice and clam soup

Sopa juliana

Ingredients for 6 servings:

400 g (14 oz) rice

1 kg (2 lbs) large clams

200 g (7 oz) onions

1 1/2 dl (1/3 pint) oil

1 bay leaf

1 sprig parsley

1 1/2 litres (3 pints) water

Salt

Easy

• Preparation time:
  45 minutes.

1. Heat the water, lightly salted and flavoured with the bay leaf. When it comes to the boil, add the clams (open and cleaned of sand) and boil for ten or twelve minutes.

2. Remove the clams and strain the stock. Return the stock to the pan in which it was boiled and add the rice, which should boil for between eighteen and twenty minutes.

3. Heat the oil in a frying pan and lightly fry the previously chopped onion and parsley. . . Then add the contents of the frying pan to the pan in which the rice has boiled, add salt to taste where necessary and add the clams (with or without their shells, as preferred). Stir the soup, turn up the heat and boil rapidly, then remove from the heat and serve.

Suggestion

If you do not have fresh vegetables, you can buy dried vegetables known as «julienne»; in this case they should be soaked for a few hours.

If it is made in a pressure cooker, the cooking time will be much shorter, and the water should only cover two thirds.

Stuffed potatoes

Patatas rellenas

Ingredients for 4 servings:

1 1/2 kg (3 lbs) medium sized potatoes

200 g (7 oz) minced meat

2 eggs

1 clove garlic

Parsley

1 onion

Olive oil or butter

1/2 pepper

2 tomatoes

Flour

1/2 small glass white wine

Stock or water

Complicated

• Preparation time:
  50 minutes.

1. Peel and wash the potatoes. Remove the pulp with a suitable utensil, leaving a hole in the inside.

2. Prepare a mixture with the minced meat, onion, peeled and seedless tomatoes, pepper, garlic and parsley, all very finely chopped.

3. Season with salt and add a beaten egg.

4. Fill the potatoes with this mixture. Then coat in flour and the other beaten egg.

5. Fry in oil with a little butter, or just in oil.

6. Once fried, place in a saucepan with the boiling stock or water, mixing with a little white wine.

7. Boil until soft, but taking care that they do not crumble. Serve with the same sauce.

Photo: Stuffed potatoes

Fishermen's style rice

Arroz a la marinera

Ingredients for 4 servings:

400 g (14 oz) rice

1 1/2 kg (3 lbs) rock-fish (scorpion fish, rose fish)

300 g (10 1/2 oz) potatoes

300 g (10 1/2 oz) onions

1/2 head of garlic

1 1/2 dl (1/3 pint) oil

6 g (1/5 oz) paprika

4 strands saffron, 2 bay leaves

Salt, 1 1/2 l (2 1/2 pints) water

Somewhat difficult

- Preparation time:
  1 hour.

1. Pour the water, slightly salted, into a pan and heat together with the bay leaves and meanwhile, separately, in half the oil, lightly fry the sliced onion, potatoes and garlic. When the fried mixture is golden, add half the paprika and fry for a minute or a minute and a half. Add the fried mixture to the hot water and cook for 30 to 40 minutes.

2. Clean the fish, cut into portions and add to the stock when the latter has been boiling for over half an hour (step 1). When the fish is cooked, remove the bay leaves, strain the stock and put the vegetables and fish on one side.

3. Into an appropriate pan, i.e. a paella dish, pour the rest of the oil and lightly fry the tomato and the rest of the paprika. After seven or eight minutes, add the rice and lightly fry for a minute and a half or two minutes more, taking care to prevent it from burning.

4. Pour into the paella dish 1 litre of the strained stock in which the fish was boiled, and boil for ten minutes. Once this time is up, add the saffron and lower the temperature for nine or ten minutes longer.

5. Remove the paella dish from the heat and leave to stand for at least another five minutes before serving.

Baked rice

Arroz al horno

Ingredients for 4 servings:

400 g (14 oz) rice

125 g (4 1/2 oz) chick-peas

200 g (7 oz) potatoes

300 g (10 1/2 oz) tomatoes

1 whole head of garlic

2 loose cloves of garlic

1 dl (1/5 pint) oil

1 l (2 pints) water or stock

Strands of saffron, salt

Complicated

- Preparation time:
  40 minutes (if the chick-peas are already cooked).

1. Boil the chick-peas (soaked for at least twelve hours beforehand) in salted water and remove when soft. Thereupon, add salt according to taste and a few strands of saffron.

2. In a frying pan, lightly fry half the tomatoes and two cloves of garlic. Next, add the potato, cut into slices, and the head of garlic and fry lightly. Add the rice, which is also lightly fried, taking care that it does not become over-fried or burnt.

3. Place the lightly fried mixture, including the rice and the chick-peas, into an ovenproof earthenware casserole dish. Add a litre of water or stock; add salt to taste and more saffron. Spread the rice around the casserole dish and place the head of garlic in the centre, garnish decoratively with the tomatoes not used in the fried mixture, cut into slices.

4. Place in a pre-heated oven at 200º C, and bake for twenty minutes. Leave to stand for five minutes before serving.

Tip

Housewives who have made a chick-pea stew often use the left-over chick-peas to make baked rice the following day. In some places dried beans are used instead of chick-peas, which must also be previously soaked and boiled.

Photo: Fishermen's style rice

Paella

Ingredients for 10 servings:

1 kg (2 lbs) paella rice
2 kg (4 lbs) chicken
1 kg (2 lbs) rabbit
300 g (10 1/2 oz) tomatoes
500 g (1 lb) runner beans (of the «ferrada» or «tavella» variety)
250 g (8 oz) garrafó (butter beans)
100 g (3 1/2 oz) peppers (optional)
2 dozen mountain snails, «vaquetas» (optional)
3 1/2 dl (1/2 pint) olive oil
Strands of saffron
1 sprig rosemary (optional)
6 g (1/5 oz) paprika
Salt
3 1/2 l (7 pints) water

Very difficult,

as it is a paella for 10 cooked in the open air over a log fire.

- Preparation time:
  1 hour and 30 minutes, taking into account the preparation of the other ingredients.

1. Place the paella dish over the fire, prepared with logs, with the oil, and when it is very hot, add the chicken and rabbit, which have previously been cut into small pieces, and fry lightly until golden brown, taking care to prevent them from burning.
2. Add the peeled tomato, seedless and crushed, and the peppers cut into strips and lightly fry on a low flame for seven or eight minutes. Lightly season with salt, and when the fried mixture is almost done, add the pepper and mix with the rest of the ingredients; fry lightly taking care that it does not burn.
3. Add the water until it reaches approximately the rivets of the handles of the paella dish. The boiling time of the meat in this water will depend on the consistency of the same, but you may calculate between thirty and thirty five minutes if the chicken and rabbit are farmyard-bred.
4. Ten minutes before the end of the time calculated for boiling the meat, add the vegetables (the runner beans and butter beans), as these should turn out «al dente». This is also the time to add the snails, which will have been purged the day before.
5. Add hot water to replace that which has evaporated and continue to boil for three or four minutes so that the new water may become suitably mixed with the original. Add the saffron, add salt to taste and continue to boil for another five minutes.
6. When the paella is fully boiling, add the rice, which is distributed equally around the pan. It should boil for five or six minutes over a high flame, then lower the heat gradually, taking into account the warnings given in the prologue.
7. When the rice is boiled it should be dry and practically loose, and for this purpose the pan is placed on the ground, if possible directly on top of the earth, for a few minutes, during which the grains of rice will absorb the final traces of stock before serving.

Photo: Paella

Baked eggs

Huevos cocidos

Ingredients for 4 servings:

4 eggs

100 g (3 1/2 oz) butter

Salt

Easy

- Preparation time:
  15 minutes.

1. Grease four individual dishes or one larger ovenproof serving dish with plenty of butter.
2. Break the eggs over them. Salt and bake in the oven until done, but taking into account that the yolk should remain soft.

Suggestion

They may be accompanied by «Kidneys in sherry» (see recipe), grated cheese, chopped ham, etc.

Eggs with white sauce

Huevos con bechamel

Ingredients for 4 servings:

4 eggs

Tomato sauce

White sauce

Butter

Easy

- Preparation time:
  15 minutes.

1. Boil the eggs for five minutes.
2. Shell and cut into two lengthways or leave whole. Place over a tomato pure or sauce.
3. Make a white sauce (see recipe) and cover the eggs with it.
4. Place on top a few knobs of butter and put in a hot oven for five minutes. Serve immediately.

Eggs with cured ham

Huevos con jamón

Ingredients for 4 servings:

4 eggs

Cured ham, chopped

4 slices bread

Olive oil

Salt

Tomato sauce

Easy

- Preparation time:
  15 minutes.

1. Cut the slices of bread, either round or into any other shape you like. Fry rapidly in very hot oil to prevent them from becoming hard.
2. Lightly fry the ham, chopped into small squares, in oil and place a little on top of each slice of fried bread.
3. Fry or poach the eggs (boil in water without the shell).
4. Place an egg on top of each slice of fried bread and ham. Serve accompanied with tomato sauce.

Photo: Eggs with cured ham

Potato omelette

Tortilla española

Ingredients for 4 servings:
1 kg (2 lbs) potatoes
5 eggs
Olive oil
1 teaspoon salt
250 g (8 oz) onion

Easy

• Preparation time:
40 minutes

1. Peel the potatoes, wash and cut into fine slices. Season with salt and add to the pre-heated oil in the frying pan.
2. If you want onion in the omelette, chop and add to the potatoes. Stir it all with a fork. This operation should be repeated frequently to soften the potatoes.
3. When the potatoes are soft, remove with the skimmer, draining off the oil, and add to the beaten eggs in a bowl.
4. With the bottom of the frying pan slightly oiled, add the eggs and potatoes. Leave for a while, moving with light shakes of the frying pan, and turn over with the help of a plate or a lid.
5. Once lightly golden on both sides, place in a round serving dish.

Asparagus omelette

Tortilla de espárragos

Ingredients for 4 servings:
4 eggs
1/2 kg (1 lb) asparagus (fresh or tinned)
Olive oil
Salt

Easy

• Preparation time:
15 minutes.

1. If the asparagus are fresh they should be boiled in hot water and seasoned with salt afterwards. If they are tinned, this is not necessary.
2. Beat the eggs and add to them the chopped asparagus.
3. Place the mixture in a frying pan with very little oil and make the omelette.

Strewed omelette

Tortilla guisada

Ingredients for 4 servings:
1 potato omelette
1 glass white wine
2 tomatoes
1 pepper
Stock or water

Easy

• Preparation time:
70 minutes.

1. Make the potato omelette (see recipe).
2. Boil for approximately half an hour in water or stock, to which the wine is added, covering the omelette. When it comes to the boil, add the tomato and the pepper, the latter in large pieces.
3. Remove carefully, as it crumbles easily, and place in a serving dish. Place the peppers on top. Sieve the stock and pour over the omelette.

Photo: Potato omelette

Meatballs

Albóndigas

Ingredients for 4 servings:

1/2 kg (1 lb) minced meat
2 eggs
2 tablespoons chopped onion
Parsley
Salt
Olive oil
Breadcrumbs
50 g (1 3/4 oz) ham
2 tomatoes
1 small glass white wine

Easy

- Preparation time:
  40 minutes.

1. To the minced meat add the ham, a tablespoon of onion and a few sprigs of parsley, all finely chopped.
2. Beat the eggs and add to the meat; add enough breadcrumbs to make it thick but not too dry.
3. Make small balls with this mixture and fry in hot oil. Place in a saucepan.
4. In the oil used to fry the meatballs, or part of it if there is a lot, lightly fry another spoonful of chopped onion and two chopped tomatoes, skinned and seedless. Add the white wine and pour the mixture over the meatballs.
5. Cook the latter, adding a little water where necessary. Serve hot in their own sauce.

Roast meat

Carne asada

Ingredients for 4 servings:

1 kg (2 lbs) beef (from the round or any other part of the leg)
1/2 onion
Garlic
Parsley
Olive oil
1 glass white wine
1 teaspoon butter or 50 g (1 3/4 oz) pork fat

Easy

- Preparation time:
  1 hour.

1. Truss the meat and season with garlic, parsley and salt, all crushed in a mortar. It is best to carry out this operation the day before.
2. Grease with butter or place a few strips of fat on top; place in a baking dish, cover with the white wine and place a few pieces of onion around the dish.
3. Place in the oven, covered with greased foil to prevent it from burning. Halfway through the cooking time, turn it over.
4. To find out when it is cooked, pierce with a needle or a fork. It will go through easily if the meat is done. It can be served with pulses, potatoes or croquettes.

Roast kid

Cabrito asado

Ingredients for 4 servings:

1 kg (2 lbs) kid
1/2 onion
Garlic
Parsley
Olive oil
Peppercorns
Thyme
Mint
Bay leaf
1 small glass white wine
Salt

Easy

- Preparation time:
  1 hour.

1. Season the kid with salt, crushed garlic and parsley.
2. Place in an ovenproof dish, cover with white wine and oil and place around it a few thyme, mint and a bay leaves. Cover with onion slices.
3. Put in the oven to roast, placing greased foil on top to prevent it from burning.
4. Strain the sauce before serving.

Photo: Roast meat

Offal stew

Chanfaina

Ingredients for 4 servings:

Veal or lamb offal
(lungs, liver, etc)

Onion

Garlic

Parsley

Paprika

Herbs

Oil

1/2 kg (1 lb) potatoes

Easy

• Preparation time:
  3 hours.

1. Boil the heart and lungs for two hours as they are very tough.
2. Once boiled, cut into pieces and fry lightly with the rest of the chopped offal. Place in a casserole dish.
3. In the oil used to fry the offal, lightly fry the finely chopped onion, garlic and parsley. Then add the potatoes, peeled and cut into medium sized pieces. When it is all lightly fried, pour over the offal.
4. Add water and a bay leaf, mint and thyme. Boil until all the ingredients are tender. Serve runny in a deep serving dish.

Lamb cutlets in batter

Chuletas de cordero con batín

Ingredients for 4 servings:

16 lamb cutlets

Salt, garlic

Flour, olive oil

1 teaspoon baking powder

1 small coffee cup milk

1 glass sherry or white wine

Complicated

• Preparation time:
  40 minutes.

1. Loosen the bone from the cutlets, but without separating the meat completely.
2. Fry in moderately hot oil; place in a serving dish and pour on sherry or white wine.
3. Dissolve in the hot milk the baking powder, a little salt and enough flour to make a fairly thick batter.
4. Coat the meat of the cutlets in this batter, leaving the bone clean. Fry again in very hot oil to cover the cutlet well.
5. Place in a serving dish and serve accompanied by French fried potatoes.

Sweetbread stew

Mollejas guisadas

Ingredients for 4 servings:

1/2 kg (1 lb) sweetbreads

50 g (1 3/4 oz) pork fat

Leeks or onions

1 clove garlic

Parsley

Salt

1 small glass white wine

Stock or water

Easy

• Preparation time:
  40 minutes.

1. Clean and wash the sweetbreads thoroughly. Soak for an hour in stock or fresh water.
2. Boil with water, onion, garlic, parsley, white wine and salt. Add a little melted fat in which the paprika is dissolved.
3. Boil the sweetbreads until they are done.

Alternative version:

Boil the sweetbreads, without adding the pork fat or paprika, for 4 or 5 minutes. Take them out and remove the fat and the skin covering them. Cut into pieces and fry in oil or butter. They may also be coated in flour, egg and breadcrumbs. Once fried, bake in the oven for a few minutes and serve.

Kidneys in sherry

Riñones al jerez

Ingredients for 4 servings:

3/4 kg (1 1/2 lbs) kidneys

Olive oil or butter

50 g (1 3/4 oz) cured ham

2 tablespoons chopped onion

Parsley

1 clove garlic

1/2 small glass sherry

Pepper

Salt

Easy

• Preparation time:
  50 minutes.

1. Clean the kidneys thoroughly, cut them into small pieces and lightly fry in a frying pan on high heat in a tablespoon of oil; stir well and place in a colander to drain for half an hour.
2. In the oil or butter, or both, lightly fry small squares of ham, onion, garlic and the sherry.
3. To this fried mixture add the strained kidneys and a little pepper. Leave to boil for around five minutes.
4. They may be served with white rice.

Meatloaf

Rollo de carne

Ingredients for 4 servings:

1/2 kg (1 lb) minced meat
1/4 kg (1/2 lb) minced liver
4 eggs
4 tablespoons breadcrumbs
50 g (1 3/4 oz) bacon
1 onion
50 g (1 3/4 oz) cured ham
Garlic
Parsley
Olive oil
Salt
Tomato sauce

Complicated

- Preparation time:
  50 minutes.

1. Season the meat and liver with salt, crushed garlic and parsley. Boil two eggs.
2. Add half a chopped onion, two beaten eggs, the ham and bacon, also chopped, and the breadcrumbs.
3. Make a roll, placing the boiled eggs one at each end, stuffed inside the meat.
4. Fry this roll until golden in abundant hot oil. Place in a baking dish with a few slices of onion and a few tablespoons of stock or water. Cover with greased foil to prevent it from burning.
5. Bake until done. To test, stick a needle through. If it comes out clean, then it is done.
6. Leave to cool and cut into slices. Serve with tomato sauce

Suggestion

If you want a smoother taste, you can add a potato boiled in salted water. Put it through a grinder or mash it and add at the beginning to the minced meat.

Roast suckling pig

Cochinillo asado

Ingredients for 4 servings:

1 suckling pig
3 cloves garlic
Salt
Parsley
Pepper
Bay leaf
Oregano
Mint
1/4 kg (1/2 lb) butter

Easy

- Preparation time:
  1 hour.

1. Clean the suckling pig and remove the fat. Season with garlic, salt, parsley and pepper.
2. Soak for a day in water with a bay leaf, oregano, mint and any other herb of your choice.
3. Remove from the water, drain and grease with butter. Place on a spit and rotate until it becomes golden without browning. If you do not have a spit, it can be roasted in the oven.
4. Serve it up whole on the table, accompanied with any sauce suitable for roasts (see sauces).

Photo: Roast suckling pig

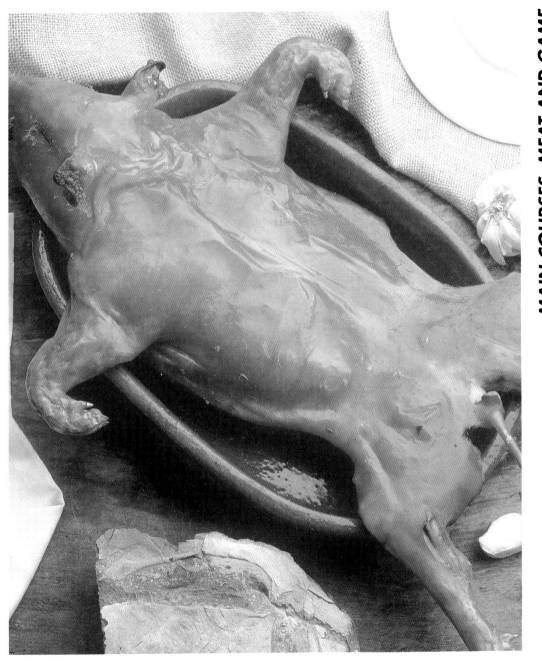

Hare or rabbit stew

Liebre o conejo guisado

Ingredients for 4 servings:

1 hare, 1 lemon, 1 onion

4 rashers bacon or cured ham

2 cloves garlic, 1 bay leaf

Salt, parsley

Olive oil, paprika

Mixed herbs

Complicated

• Preparation time:
  1 hour.

1. Clean the hare, leaving in the liver; season with salt, garlic and parsley crushed in a mortar. Leave to marinade overnight, or a little longer, and cut into pieces.

2. In hot oil, lightly fry the chopped onion, which is then spread around the bottom of a cake tin; on top of the onion, place thin rashers of bacon.

3. Place the pieces of hare on top of the bacon, together with the liver; cover with a squeeze of lemon juice, season with pepper, pour over it a small coffee cup of boiling stock or water and leave to boil on a high gas.

4. If the sauce dries up, add more water, taking into account that the less water we add, the more substantial the meat will be.

5. Thicken the sauce with the minced livers. The bacon may be removed before serving.

Chick surprise

Pollo sorpresa

Ingredients for 4 servings:

1 chicken, olive oil

2 tablespoons butter

1 large carrot

1 medium onion

Parsley, salt

1 clove garlic, 1 bay leaf

1 small glass dry white wine

Potato purée

2 tablespoons grated cheese

Easy

• Preparation time:
  50 minutes.

1. Once the chicken is clean, season with salt, garlic and parsley. Cut into pieces and boil with the butter, wine, carrot, bay leaf and onion.

2. When it is boiled, place in a small heap and cover with potato purée. Decorate it also with purée by placing it in a piping bag with a rose nozzle.

3. Cover with grated cheese and bake in a hot oven for a few minutes. The sauce from boiling the chicken is served separately.

Truffled chicken

Pollo trufado

Ingredients for 4 servings:

1 chicken

1/2 kg (1 lb) veal, lean pork and cured ham

1 onion, 1 clove garlic

Parsley, 1 carrot

1 beef bone, 1 veal trotter

1 piece ham 100 g (3 1/2 oz)

1 small tin truffles, salt

1 small glass sherry

Complicated

• Preparation time:
  2 1/2 hours.

1. Bone the thoroughly cleaned chicken; first the wing area, then make a cut in the spine and bone the rest.

2. In this cut, place the filling made from the veal, lean pork and ham, all finely chopped and seasoned with salt, spices if desired, chopped truffles and covered with the sherry. Once stuffed, sew up the back.

3. In cold water, place a few pieces of onion, the garlic, the parsley, all the bones (trotter, ham…) the chicken giblets and the carrot.

4. Once the stock has boiled for an hour, place the chicken in it. When the latter is cooked, serve cold cut into slices. Serve in a sauceboat.

Photo: Truffled chicken

Bilbao style cod

Bacalao a la bilbaína

Ingredients for 4 servings:
1/2 kg (1 lb) cod
1 chilli
1 tablespoon butter
2 tablespoons oil
1 1/2 onions
1 clove garlic
100 g (3 1/2 oz) cured ham
2 eggs
1 teaspoon sugar

Complicated

• Preparation time:
50 minutes.

1. If the cod is salted, cut it into pieces and soak for eight to ten hours, together with the chilli.
2. In the butter and oil, fry an onion and the ham, all finely chopped. Once golden, pour in a cup of water and add the chopped chilli and cook for a few minutes.
3. Sieve this fried mixture and add two hard boiled egg yolks, well broken up, and the sugar.
4. Boil the cod in water with onion and garlic. When it is almost cooked, remove the bones and add the sauce prepared previously.
5. Leave the cod to boil in the sauce for a few minutes.

Cod «pil-pil»

Bacalao al pil-pil

Ingredients for 4 servings:
1/2 kg (1 lb) cod
1 small onion
2 cloves garlic, 1 bay leaf
1 small glass white wine
1/4 l (1/2 pint) milk

Complicated

• Preparation time:
1 hour.

1. Cut the cod into pieces and soak for eight to ten hours.
2. Boil in water for around 5 minutes.
3. In hot oil, fry a small onion and the garlic for approximately ten minutes until golden, taking care to prevent them from burning; then add the bay leaf.
4. Drain the water from the cod and lightly fry with the onion and white wine for another ten minutes.
5. Take the cod out of the frying pan and place in an earthenware casserole dish. Add to the onion a small coffee cup of water, where possible that used to boil the cod.
6. Strain the latter and pour over the cod, which is left to simmer on a low heat for half an hour. As the sauce evaporates, add a little milk, moving the casserole dish but without stirring the fish.
7. Serve in the same casserole dish, sprinkling with parsley whilst it is still boiling.

Baked bream

Besugo al horno

Ingredients:
1 bream
Salt
3 tablespoons olive oil
Parsley
1 lemon
1 onion
Stock or water
1 small glass white wine

Easy

• Preparation time:
40 minutes.

1. Once the bream is clean, make two or three cuts in the back and season with salt. In each cut, place a slice of lemon or onion and place in the fish pan.
2. Cover with boiling oil and white wine, adding a little water to the fish pan to prevent the fish from burning. On top or around, place a few large pieces of onion and a few sprigs of parsley.
3. Bake in the oven until well done and serve very hot straight out of the oven.

Photo: Bilbao style cod

Squid in their own ink

Calamares en su tinta

Ingredients for 4 servings:

1/2 kg (1 lb) squid

2 tablespoons chopped onion

1 clove garlic

Salt

1 small glass red wine

Flour, paprika

1 tablespoon grated or powdered chocolate

Easy

- Preparation time: 50 minutes.

1. Clean the squid thoroughly, putting the ink sacs to one side.
2. Cut into pieces and lightly fry in a frying pan. Then add the chopped onion, the wine, the chocolate powder and a little paprika. Place it all in a saucepan.
3. Add the ink sacs, pounded in a mortar with a little cooking salt and water, to the squid.
4. Leave to boil, add the necessary water. Serve in all its sauce.

Note.

If you find it complicated to remove the ink from the squid, it can be bought ready prepared for use.

Fish stew

Caldereta

Ingredients for 4 servings:

1 kg (2 lbs) assorted fish and seafood

1 onion

Parsley

2 sweet red peppers

1 small coffee cup tomato purée

3 walnuts or 6 almonds

1 small glass sherry

Olive oil

Salt

2 cloves

Easy

- Preparation time: 50 minutes.

1. Mix the fish, cleaned and split, with the seafood. If there are clams, open them previously in water to clean them of sand.
2. Mix the chopped onion, parsley, peppers, and nuts, crushed in a mortar, and the sherry. Season with salt, and add the spices, if desired, and the tomato purée.
3. In a saucepan, place a layer of this mixture and another of fish and seafood, and so on until finishing with a layer of the mixture.
4. Cover hermetically and leave to simmer on a low heat until all the ingredients are done.

Conger eel in parsley sauce

Congrio en salsa verde

Ingredients for 4 servings:

4 thick slices conger eel

Flour

Salt

Olive oil

1 teaspoon chopped onion

Parsley

1 clove garlic

2 small coffee cups stock or water

Easy

- Preparation time: 40 minutes.

1. Season the conger eel with salt. Coat in flour and fry in very hot oil. Place in a saucepan.
2. In very hot oil, lightly fry two tablespoons of flour and a finely chopped onion. Once the latter is golden, add two small coffee cups of stock or water and boil for a few minutes. Season with salt and add a few sprigs of parsley previously ground in a mortar.
3. Pour this sauce over the conger eel and boil it all together for a few minutes for the fish to absorb the flavour. Serve in its sauce.

Photo: Conger eel in parsley sauce

Asturian style lamprey

Lamprea a la asturiana

Ingredients for 4 servings:

1 lamprey
1 glass white wine
1 teaspoon grated or powdered chocolate
Olive oil, 1 clove garlic, parsley
1 tablespoon chopped onion

Easy

- Preparation time:
  40 minutes.

1. Wash the lamprey thoroughly in hot water. Make a few cuts in the back and remove the insides, as they are very bitter. Take care to collect the blood which comes out and place the liver on one side.
2. Fry the chopped onion, garlic and parsley in oil; then add a glass of white wine, the blood collected, the chocolate powder and the chopped liver of the lamprey.
3. Pour this mixture over the lamprey. Season with salt and simmer on a low heat in a saucepan, well sealed with brown wrapping paper and the lid. If the sauce is not enough for boiling, add a few tablespoons of water.
4. Serve in its sauce after straining.

Baked hake or bream

Merluza o besugo al horno

Ingredients for 4 servings:

1 kg (2 lbs) hake (from the tail end) or bream
3 tablespoons butter, pepper
1/4 l (1/2 pint) milk, salt
Breadcrumbs, lemon

Easy

- Preparation time:
  3 hours.

1. Clean the fish and remove the skin. Season with salt and pepper and cover with a squeeze of lemon juice.
2. Pour the milk into an an ovenproof dish and place the fish on top; leave to stand for two hours.
3. Once this time is up, sprinkle with breadcrumbs and parsley, place on top a few knobs of butter and bake in the oven until the milk evaporates and the fish is cooked.
4. Once this time is up, sprinkle with breadcrumbs and parsley, place on top a few knobs of butter and bake in the oven until the milk evaporates and the fish is cooked.

Alternative version:

You may leave out the breadcrumbs and the parsley, and substitute the milk with water, white wine and a few pieces of onion. In this case there is no need to leave it to stand for two hours, it can be baked straight away, which means that the preparation time is considerably reduced.

Fish in brine

Pescado en escabeche

Ingredients for 4 servings:

1 kg (2 lbs) fish, olive oil
6 cloves garlic, 2 bay leaves
1 large onion, flour, vinegar

Easy

- Preparation time:
  40 minutes.

1. Wash and clean the fish thoroughly; season with salt, coat in flour and fry in abundant oil.
2. In this same oil, fry the garlic and a large onion, cut into pieces, until golden.
3. In an earthenware casserole dish, place the fish and pour over it the oil with the onions and the garlic, adding the bay leaf and enough vinegar to cover all the fish.
4. Boil for two minutes; remove from the heat and cover well, placing a piece of brown wrapping paper under the lid to make it fit tightly. Once it takes the flavour it is ready to serve.

Photo: Fish in brine

Clams à la marinière

Almejas a la marinera

Ingredients for 4 servings:

1 kg (2 lbs) clams
1 tablespoon butter
2 tablespoons olive oil
3 tablespoons chopped onion
1 clove garlic
Parsley
Salt
2 tablespoons flour
1 small glass white wine

Easy

- Preparation time:
  30 minutes.

1. Wash the clams thoroughly and boil with enough water to cover them and the glass of wine. Skim from time to time.
2. Once open, remove with the skimmer, after having stirred well to remove any sand which may be in them. Leave the water to stand.
3. In the butter, mixed with two tablespoons of oil, fry until golden the chopped onion, garlic and parsley, also chopped. Add the flour and lightly fry for a little longer.
4. Add the clams, pour in the water used to boil them, taking care not to let any sand fall in. Serve hot.

Baked scallops or «pilgrim's shells»

Vieiras o conchas de peregrino al horno

Ingredients for 4 servings:

8 scallops
4 tablespoons chopped onion
1 clove garlic
1 sprig parsley
Pepper
Clove
1 beaten egg
2 tablespoons breadcrumbs
1 tablespoon oil or 2 of butter
Salt

Easy

- Preparation time:
  30 minutes.

1. Remove the molluscs from the shells, cut into pieces and mix with the rest of the ingredients to make a paste to fill the shells.
2. Bake in an ovenproof dish with a little water at the bottom. Serve hot.

Mountain style trout

Truchas a la montañesa

Ingredients for 4 servings:

4 trout
1/2 onion
Peppercorns
1 bay leaf
Flour
1 small glass white wine
Olive oil

Easy

- Preparation time:
  40 minutes.

1. Clean the trout and season with salt two or three hours before cooking.
2. Boil in a casserole dish, preferably earthenware, covering with the white wine, adding a small coffee cup of water, a few pieces of onion, two peppercorns and the bay leaf.
3. Once cooked, leave to cool and strain the sauce.
4. In the oil, fry a tablespoon of flour until golden, then add the strained sauce. Leave to boil for two or three minutes. Pour over the trout and serve.

Photo: Clams à la marinière

Rice pudding with caramel

Arroz con leche al caramelo

Ingredients for 4 servings:

1 bowlful rice
1 small coffee cup water
2 cups milk
3 tablespoons butter
Sugar
Stick of cinnamon
Lemon
Salt

Complicated

- Preparation time:
  40 minutes.

1. Pour the rice into boiling water. Add the butter and a little cinnamon, either stick or ground.
2. When the water has boiled dry, gradually add the milk, according to how dry the rice is, and a small piece of lemon, whilst continuing to simmer on a low heat. Add a pinch of salt.
3. When it is cooked, add the sugar according to taste, and leave to cool for a while. When the surface is slightly set, sprinkle with sugar.
4. Serve lukewarm, almost cold.

Apple sponge or cake

Pastel de manzana

Ingredients:

100 g (3 1/2 oz) butter
100 g (3 1/2 oz) sugar
1/2 sachet baking powder
100 g (3 1/2 oz) flour
2 eggs
1/2 kg (1 lb) apples
Icing sugar

Easy

- Preparation:
  50 minutes.

1. Make a mixture with the butter, sugar, eggs, and baking powder dissolved in a tablespoon of milk. Work in well.
2. With half the mixture, line a greased mould which should be round and smooth.
3. Peel the apples, remove the core, cut into quarters and then into fine slices.
4. Spread the apple over the dough in the mould, top with sugar and cover with the rest of the dough.
5. Bake in a medium hot oven. Test by sticking in a needle. If the latter comes out clean, then it is ready.

Swiss roll

Brazo de gitano

Ingredients:

3 eggs
3 tablespoons flour
3 tablespoons sugar
Confectioner's custard

Complicated

- Preparation time:
  1 hour.

1. Beat the egg whites until stiff. Beat the yolks also and mix with the whites; add the sugar. When it is all mixed, gradually add the flour.
2. Pour this mixture into a greased mould. Place in a hot oven, covered with foil to prevent it from burning on top. Test by sticking in a needle. If the latter comes out clean, then it is ready.
3. Leave to cool and turn out of the mould. While the sponge is still lukewarm, spread over it the confectioner's custard (see recipe) and roll up. Wrap in white paper and leave to cool.
4. Once cool, place on a serving dish and decorate, either with meringue, chocolate cream or butter mixed with sugar and squeezed through a piping bag with a rose nozzle.

Photo: Swiss roll

Fruit sundae

Copa de frutas

Ingredients:

Assorted fruit

Nuts (almonds, walnuts, hazelnuts etc.)

Sugar, brandy

Fizzy lemonade (clear type)

Whipped cream or meringue

Easy

- Preparation time:
  3 hours.

1. Clean and peel the fruit and cut into pieces.
2. Grind the nuts and add to the fruit. To this mixture add clear fizzy lemonade or sugar according to taste, and a little brandy or other liqueur. Leave to soak for two hours.
3. Serve in sundae glasses and on top of each, add a blob of whipped cream or meringue.

Compote

Compota

Ingredients for 4 servings:

8 pears or apples

200 g (7 oz) sugar

1/2 glass sherry

Stick of cinnamon

Easy

- Preparation time:
  20 minutes.

1. Peel the fruit and cut each piece into quarters. Boil in sufficient water to cover the fruit, the sherry, a few sticks of cinnamon and plenty of sugar.
2. When the fruit is soft, remove from the heat and leave to cool.

Notes.

The cinnamon and sherry may be left out according to the taste of the dinner guests.

Confectioners' custard

Crema pastelera

Ingredients:

2 tablespoons flour

3 tablespoons sugar

1 or 2 egg yolks

Lemon rind, boiling milk

Cinnamon

Easy

- Preparation time:
  15 minutes.

1. Mix well the flour, sugar, egg yolks and enough milk to make a light mixture. Add the lemon rind and cinnamon.
2. Cook on a low heat for around ten minutes, stirring constantly to prevent it from sticking or curdling.
3. Spread over a serving dish, dust with cinnamon and place in a moderate oven to keep warm whilst we prepare the sponge or cake in which we are going to use it.

Fritters

Churros

Ingredients:

1 bowlful flour

1 bowlful water

1 thin slice lemon

Salt, sugar, olive oil

Easy

- Preparation time:
  30 minutes.

1. Boil the slightly salted water with the lemon.
2. When it comes to the boil, remove the lemon and add the flour, stirring until it becomes a smooth dough. Remove from the heat and knead until very smooth.
3. Place the slightly dampened dough in a churro or fritter machine and make the churros, which are placed on a floured surface.
4. Fry immediately in hot oil. Drain and place on a serving dish. If you wish, dust them with sugar. Serve freshly fried.

Photo: Confectioners' custard

Creme caramel

Flan

Ingredients for 4 servings:

4 eggs

4 small coffee cups milk

6 tablespoons sugar

Cinnamon

Easy

• Preparation time:
  30 minutes.

1. Place in a mould two tablespoons of sugar and with this make caramel. Spread the liquid caramel around the mould so that the whole inside surface is covered. Leave to cool.
2. Beat the eggs (or just the yolks if you want it smoother), and add four tablespoons of sugar, the milk and the cinnamon. Mix well and pour into the cooled mould.
3. Place, well covered, in a bain-marie in a normal saucepan or in a pressure cooker until it is set; without removing from the water, place in the oven for a few moments.
4. Leave to cool and turn out onto a serving dish or glass plate.

Fried milk

Leche frita

Ingredients:

1/2 l (1 pint) milk

4 or 5 tablespoons flour

2 tablespoons butter

Lemon rind

Stick or ground cinnamon

2 eggs, sugar, olive oil

Easy

• Preparation time:
  50 minutes.

1. Mix the flour into the cold milk, add a piece of lemon rind or a small slice of lemon and a stick of cinnamon.
2. Bring to the boil, stirring continuously, and add the butter. Leave to simmer for at least 15 minutes. When it is almost done, add the sugar according to taste.
3. Once cooked, spread over a damp serving dish to cool, removing the lemon and cinnamon beforehand.
4. When it has cooled, cut into large squares, which will come away easily from the serving dish if the milk is well cooked.
5. Coat these squares in flour and egg and fry in hot oil. Drain well and dust with sugar.

Custard

Natillas

Ingredients for 4 servings:

4 egg yolks, cinnamon

4 coffee cups milk

4 tablespoons sugar

Easy

• Preparation time:
  15 minutes.

1. Beat the yolks and mix with the milk, sugar and a little ground cinnamon. Cook on a low heat until it thickens, stirring constantly to prevent it from sticking or curdling. It must not boil.
2. Serve cold. You may decorate the top with a sponge finger, a biscuit or cinnamon.

French toast

Torrijas

Ingredients:

Slices of stale bread

Milk, sugar, olive oil, eggs

Easy

• Preparation time:
  15 minutes.

1. Soak the slices of bread in sugared milk. Coat in beaten egg and fry in abundant hot oil.
2. Drain and dust with sugar.

Photo: French Toast.

M

N

O

P

R

S

T

V

W

The photographs taken for this book
were done at Restraurante
Parrillada Serrano, in
Astorga. We wish to express our
gratitud for their collaboration.

Photography:
Imagen MAS

Editorial coordination:
Ángeles Llamazares Álvarez

Lay out:
Jorge Garrán Marey
Carmen García Rodríguez

Cover design:
Francisco A. Morais

Translation:
EURO:TEXT

FIFTH EDITION

© EDITORIAL EVEREST, S.A.
Carretera León-La Coruña, km 5
LEÓN (Spain)
ISBN: 84-241-2316-6
Legal deposit: LE. 308 - 2002
Printed in Spain

EDITORIAL EVERGRÁFICAS, S.L.
Carretera León-La Coruña, km. 5
LEÓN (Spain)